Free Verse Editions
Edited by Jon Thompson

BARI'S LOVE SONG

Kang Eun-Gyo

Translated by Chung Eun-Gwi

Parlor Press
Anderson, South Carolina
www.parlorpress.com

Parlor Press LLC, Anderson, South Carolina, 29621

This book is published with the support of the Literature Translation Institute of Korea (LTI Korea).

Printed in the United States of America
S A N: 2 5 4 - 8 8 7 9

Library of Congress Cataloging-in-Publication Data on File

978-1-64317-082-4 (paperback)
978-1-64317-083-1 (PDF)
978-1-64317-084-8 (ePub)

1 2 3 4 5

Cover design by David Blakesley.
Cover photo by Yohan Cho on Unsplash.
Printed on acid-free paper.

Parlor Press, LLC is an independent publisher of scholarly and trade titles in print and multimedia formats. This book is available in paperback and ebook formats from Parlor Press on the World Wide Web at http://www.parlorpress.com or through online and brick-and-mortar bookstores. For submission information or to find out about Parlor Press publications, write to Parlor Press, 3015 Brackenberry Drive, Anderson, South Carolina, 29621, or email editor@parlorpress.com.

Contents

Contents

Translator's Preface

Chung Eun-Gwi

> *"Let all sadness leave us with these songs."*

In her early career, Kang marked nihilism as the departure of her poetic imagination. The poet, in response to the turmoil of the world and modern Koran history full of violence and violations of human rights, struggled to build her poetry in a house of nothing-ness. With *Bari's Love Song*, the poet echoes the voice of a sorceress, a female shaman who treats the sadness, suffering, loss, and pain of all people. From the private losses of the poet to the universal songs of losses and love, *Bari's Love Song* covers the modern history of Korea in the forms of songs and recollections. In Korean folk literature, Bari is the name of a princess who was abandoned as soon as she was born just because she was the seventh daughter of a King with no son. In the meantime the King and Queen became critically ill and Bari, the abandoned princess, traveled to the underworld to get medicine. It features Bari as the agent of action, of hope, of love. The poet, in her love songs borrowing the voice of Bari, invites readers to the scenes and spots that filled their days and years with love and revolution in modern Korean history. Demonstrating her sustained concerns and affections for forces of life, this poetry book shapes a certain communal voice for a new world beyond loss and sadness. Bari's love songs are the songs of the earliest abandoned and the most forgotten. With these songs, the poet seems to say, these are the final version of all sorrow and loss. Let all sadness leave us. Let's go to the next port.

Bari's Love Song

Abel Bookstore

Probably you will see there,
on a pale blue wooden signboard, the word "life"
standing on tiptoe, touching the evening starlight.

Behind the word a hill will be pouting its lips
or a dream-road will be shaking out its golden hair.

If you push open the stubborn door with both hands and walk in,
you will see a threshold trampling on secondhand books groaning
with all the weight of the world in its arms

If you approach the tortuous staircase
eyes will come down toward you hesitantly.

At the top of the staircase a royal azalea
looking down as if terrified toward the bottom with a pale
    white face

Perhaps you will then see
people carefully taking out cliffs like notebooks
and putting them on the table,
while on utterly worn-out chairs beneath the petals, light-pink
    shadows will
settle noisily.

Ah, do you know that place,
where a dream-road puts a collar round the cliff's inner heart, a
place where the heart is boiling like plum-colored omija-tea,
wiping tears away secretly? Surging sleeves. Sails.
Boats floating.
Today boats will leave for some beautiful port.

Immortality

—For J

The cigarette pack you dumped.
The crumpled letter you dumped.
The disposable paper cup you dumped.
The gum wrapper you dumped, this way thump, that way thump.
The wristwatch you dumped.
The huge memories you dumped.
The twilight you dumped.
The mirror you dumped, floating above the abyss, this way thump, that
    way thump.

Those weeds that once shone thanks to you.
Those mists dressed in sandstorms that once shone thanks to you.
Those sweat-tongues that once shone thanks to you, this way thump, that
    way thump.

The crack you dumped.
The symbol you dumped.
The three-thousand-ri-long* whale's wing you dumped, covering my flesh,
this way thump, that way thump

At the tip of an old spoon, this way thump, that way thump.
Hanging on the bosoms of fluttering things, this way thump, that way thump.

The eternity you dumped.
The faraway mother's voice you dumped.
The last page of the diary you dumped.
The summer day noon that you dumped, this way thump, that way thump.

The god you dumped.
The beliefs you dumped.
The liberation with fluttering shadow you dumped.
The freedom you dumped, lying on a dish, this way thump, that way thump.

The beef bone soup you dumped.
The steaming shelf you dumped.
The picture frame with long smoke of dreams you dumped.
The blazing desk you dumped, this way thump, that way thump.

Fluttering immortality flows along roads deep in the heart.

You, who are nowhere.
You, who are everywhere.
this way thump, three thousand *ri*.
That way thump, three thousand *ri*.

* Three thousand *ri* often metaphorically refers to Korea itself, as it
is the approximate length of the Korean Peninsula.

Hyehwa-dong

– for a certain dusk

Come there, once in a while, to that place where loaves gently lower their heads, where dusk is particularly beautiful, in late afternoons as the sunlight falls aslant there people murmur tales of love.
Then look down and see the golden sunlight walking through the large window, then hear the sunset wind gently pushing in its head

An old sycamore tree stands in front. Its leaves ripen in the twilight. Its leaves are building a huge garden in the sky.
A bird flying very slowly, fine roots are stretching their slender feet toward evening's sleep.

Come there once in a while, to that place where loaves are neatly standing beside giant memories. Starving, you climb stairs full of scratches.
Leaves begin to dream.

The Sound of Water in Baekmudong

Seated leaning against the sound of water, I gaze. I
gaze blankly, blankly.
The meandering sound of water disappears into the rocks
Meandering bent bones disappear into cliffs,

Seated leaning against the sound of water, I gaze. I
gaze blankly, blankly.
Holding a pair of wooden shoes
I gaze and gaze.

Tonight,
until all living things become holy

Love and Eternity

One love is crossing a road.
With no hesitation, it crosses noon.
From time to time that love
is carried off in a cloud bag.

Love is a moment's eternity.
Eternity is a moment of love.
One that never waits for us, or waits for extinction

One that waits, crunching and crushing.

Cherry Blossom Train

A woman, smiling, leaves the train station adrift with cherry blossom.

The cherry blossom drifts in the train station.

While the station's sunlight
ripens
gently, softly,
within the cherry blossom.

Poetry and a Golden Kiss

Filling in the blanks in the application papers
the lawyer, reaching the blank for the man's occupation,
wrote down 'Unemployed'
The woman protested, saying that he was not unemployed, he was a
   poet and once had been chairman of a quite famous organization for
   democratic activities,
The lawyer, his face glossy like a marble staircase, smiled casually, 'Legally,
   he is unemployed, those are just hobbies....'
The man at that moment became a door lacking an arm.
He became dull dust mixed with yellow dust blown from a faraway desert.
Their youthful days receding into the distance,
golden kisses,
their freedom receding into the distance,
golden kisses.
Once the divorce papers had all been filled in,
the lawyer chewed casually on his sweat and
spoke emotional words for the first time, with a sigh,
'Don't worry, incompetence or, rather, unemployment are both legally
   grounds for divorce.'
They had been summarized, into a divorce application,
the reason being that man's unemployment or, rather, incompetence.

An Envelope

One day I discovered that
it was a total of five poems you discarded before you left.
It must have been snowing at the time, the poems written with a
   fountain pen were blotted with tears.
They had been written in the 70's, during the *Yusin* dictatorship by
   President Park Chung-hee.
No telling when you wrote such poems while wandering around,
   and there was something about your younger brother there, too,
your brother who killed himself after wandering the whole country
   to claim his overdue wages.
The dream that longed for him so much
shone pale silver, wrapped round your neck,
lay deep in the valleys of a literary magazine, now faded a golden-
   yellow, wrapped in an envelope with crumpled corners inscribed
   'Progressive Alliance.'

Dreams are things that wrap, that wrap in envelopes of eternity
   piled and piled like snowflakes or teardrops.

Severe Illness

My love, who used to shout Revolution!
died murmuring revolution after falling seriously ill.

My love, who used to shout Progress!
died murmuring Progress! and holding an envelop marked 'Progressive
  Alliance' to his breast like a bouquet,.

If I die, bury me at *Gwanghwamun,*
bury me so that everyone can step on me as they pass by, he
murmured like a popular song

Revolution and progress crossed over the river,
crossed over the river from the room of this world to the room of the
  world beyond, as if
crossing a courtyard from the main room to the room on the opposite
  side crossing
from the room on the opposite side to the main room,

Walking then running, walking then stopping, walking then swimming,

Like a horse, like a dinosaur, like a monkey, like an elephant, like a fig,
  like a sleep, like a dream, like a home, like a meadow rainbow, like
  a wing

A Knife

The choking street, he disappeared and has maybe become the dusk. The knife that played life for a long time and the little guy will embrace each other and dream, a dream of loving each other. Tearing at one another's breast and bleeding they will spend the dusk. Their blanket will be soaked in blood. Their pillow will blankly watch this unforgettable scene. Oh, the choking night, the love of a man sharpening a knife.

My Street

—Commemorating Kang Eun-gyo in Advance

Today I was prescribed a three-month course of anticonvulsants so my
    life has been suspended until June 22.

I still don't know in what nook in the sides of my blood vessels my
    spasm is sitting The
spasm crawls to my tongue and licks the winding stairs of blood cells,
crawls to my arms and embraces my arm's green shawl.
The spasm crawls into my legs and tugs my left foot.
I stop walking for a moment.
Watching wet rose petals dreaming above my head
I start three months of sleep, three months of dreams.
Three raindrops dangling on the window of sleep.
The hot sound of the wheels of a rainbow coach suddenly rushing
    toward my heart.
My bones rustling even if I lie quietly like a Sunday afternoon.
A single breath shakes its ivory lips at my bedside. Rose
petals on my spine, rainbow coach,
scatter light's umbilical cord.
The sound of a rainbow coach's footsteps crunching in high-soprano are
following a silver railroad
so wait, wait
for the power pulling light's umbilical cord to seep into the sides of my
    blood vessels.
Spasms are my teacher, my poem, my last first love.

Today I was prescribed a three-month course of anticonvulsants so my
    life has been suspended until June 22.

What I Have At This Moment

What I have at this moment:
A bag too big, a coat too heavy, a shoe cabinet with too many
drawers, an expired silver train ticket, the twitching eyelids of
midnight windows, now with no way to touch them, loneliness
firmly wedged in fingernails, and, and this world, the bottom of
tenacious waves, and, and, and the trail I walked with you, the
purple pinks that bloomed along the trail, and so on, and so on,
etc., etc.

A Word

I am on the road in search of the most beautiful word on earth,
Some say it's life
Some say it's a handshake
Some say it's the shape of a road
Some say it's revolution
Some say it's the sound of spring rain
Some say it's a port
Some say it's music Some
say it's bugleweed

Some say it's a flag
Some say it's death
Some say it's coincidence
Some say it's a choice
Some say it's a glance
Some say it's bread
Some say it's love

I am on the road in search of the most beautiful word on earth,

Sometimes there are many roads
Sometimes a road does not exist
Sometimes a road ends
Sometimes a road starts
Sometimes a road is a guide
Sometimes a road is a grave
Sometimes a road is standing
Sometimes a road is lying

I am on the road in search of the most beautiful word on earth,

What would you say?
Would you say it's you?

A Longed-For Village

I am a longed-for neighborhood. I am a solitary house in that longed-for neighborhood. I am a shabby bag, I am old, old shoes. I am standing shivering in a November wind, one that opens and closes the breath of the maple tree rising in my heart,

On Sunday one who lives in the longed-for, most longed-for neighborhood comes visiting. Riding the subway wrapped in the smell of wet ginger that smiles embraced by the subway, emitting a smell of wet garlic, a smell of wet hope.

Inside him there are countless passageways. Passageways within passageways, passageways within passageways, if you open one door and go in, yet another room.

Hanging countless doors, he is coming. He
is a march of countless doors.
Countless doors prepare to open at his back then in the end do not
    open as they approach.

He is coming, having become the lofty doorframe of countless doors.

Shutters are covered by shutters,

Forever a frontier, forever salvation, hope, always arriving too late, he comes wearing a green hat like a guard. He comes with green glasses flapping. He comes with a roof of hope. He comes with green beard flapping. I advance toward the roof of hope. I erect a pylon on the green beard. I become a ceiling of hope. Lightly leaning my shoulder against a lightbulb of hope, lightly shedding tears on the power line of hope,

I am one corner in the longed-for, most longed-for neighborhood. Full of hope, I am Mother's brown wardrobe, full of hope, I am a clock the color of father's shadow, or else, full of hope, I am Grandmother's rainbow-colored net curtains. I am standing shivering in a November wind, one that opens and closes the breath of a maple tree rising in my heart, greeting him, forever a frontier, or forever salvation, or hope, or myself.

A Round Roof

Sometimes I think of such a place
Beautiful Maytime, a shy table set up in the yard, a roof painted
with wisteria flowers or a window quietly opening as if waiting for
someone, a dazzling silhouette falling from the nape of the wisteria
flowers, with a round roof there

Sometimes I think of such a place
Moby Dick laying its bleeding white back at a foot of cliff, a pair of
wisteria-colored guanaco with long eye-lashes kneeling beneath a
cactus on a cliff where waves break and looking at each other, warm
and cold currents meeting and holding hands, sometimes caught
in a dream "Innocent Steps" or "When You and I Were Young,
Maggie" coming running from far away like wet fog, with a round
roof there

Sometimes I think of such a place
Tinkerbell flapping green wings like a bridal veil and flying through
the thin sky, orange lamplight playing frivolously through the
chinks of a window smiling like a woman covering her mouth
with a hand, all shutters standing up and wrapping a lamp like the
Holy Grail, servants of the light taking off light's coat and carefully
hanging it on a green hanger, with a round roof there.

Sometimes I think of such a place
Bari laying a wisteria-colored hollyhock stem on her parents' lips,
Bari laying a wisteria-colored cosmos bloom on her parent's lips,
Bari making spring-water dance drop by drop on her parents'
breasts on a bier, with a round roof there

Sometimes I think of such a place
That woman watching ever so many movies, a professional whose
job is to care for the disabled and chattering ceaselessly, that woman
living alone, driving a very old car, saying proudly 'I will give you
a ride' as if she were driving a Benz or something, that woman's car
being white, like her heart, the color of sterility, pure, bringing all
light crashing, sometimes like tall Isadora Duncan, sometimes like

an ugly goose, like a petal, sinking in clusters there, 'As you wish, go staggering on, I will hold you!' laughing huskily, with a round roof there

Sometimes, I think of such a place
spruce, water-hemlock, and pine which never forgive despair
growing, five in the afternoon coming closest to the horizon,
exchanging deep glances with darkness, the shadows within me
lengthening freely, and while lengthening fields embracing the
horizon, with a round roof there

Green Sleeves

The house stood at a corner
On opening the old blue wooden door and walking in
a ruddy-cheeked golden girl used to greet me,
Mary, Mary,
"Green Sleeves" used to fly like a song of the earth.

Then one day,
feeling lonesome, I visited the house again
but the song of the earth, "Green Sleeves," had vanished
and the gravel path on the corner where the earth's song, Green
    Sleeves used to fly had vanished too,
And my old comrade, *Bari, Bari,*
who used to collapse at the riverbank letting her downy hair fly,
who used to flush crimson like the earth at sunrise.

Eunpo Station

That day at Busan station sleep was falling. The wind was blowing
low, and roofs were endlessly vomiting fog, electric display boards
were turning on souls' light like disposable lighters, and chairs were
hanging their heads fully. Walking past Comet pharmacy, Galaxy
coffee shop, and the escalator with long feet, walking on

One angel was flying between the flickering red letters on
the electric display boards. The angel's wings were white and
black, the angel's eyelids black and reddish, the angel's heart as
red as could be. In her red heart, an entrance for arrivals was
hanging precipitously.

That exit for arrivals from where you, my love, come walking,
that entrance for departures from where you, my love, come
    walking, arrivals
are beautiful
arrivals' departures are beautiful

I advance. I advance toward the entrance for departures, in search
of you, my love. Holding fast to a rail, life sometimes spread out
full length above a train wheel, life's blanket is waving with rainbow
or May peony colors, the longest letter in the world is fluttering in
hope's mailbox,

A Blind Alley

I loved a blind alley. I
loved terribly my sweetheart who lived in the blind alley. A
farewell I always used to share in the blind alley,
my love's hands that I used to touch in the blind alley,
I loved the button
of the future of an endless maze.

Tonight, I summon the dreams of my love locked in the maze. I
am running around in my love's dream,
lightly leaping like grass.

The cliff where my loving love disappeared

Ah, suffocating life.

Address

On lonely nights, I keep on writing down a blue address.
Kneeling, I keep on writing.
Putting dawn on my back to send it to sleep, I keep on writing. I
mail it in an afternoon post office.

Really, there are so many windows in the post office.
Bent births pop in and out, fall over.
Bent corpses pop in and out, fall over

Pages of writing paper are screaming. Screaming
to open the bodies of bent addresses.

I also scream and scream.
Scream and scream, again and again. I
scream as I mail off my heart.
I scream as I become a window. I soar up. Flapping, flapping.

Drizzle

That curving house, the ear of that rooftop, naked, wet with rain,
Someone hanging up, hanging up high, someone hanging up high
   like a flag

Flapping flapping, flap, flap

Let's Make a Path

Let's make a path,
let's make a path that brings you toward me.
Let's plant gingko trees along the path.
Let's hang stars at the ends of the gingko tree branches
and the songs of street birds.

At the end of the gingko tree's half-closed eyes the sound of your dream,
sending flying the Milky Way's eyelids.
At the end of thegingko tree's half-closed eyes the sound of my dream,
sending the Milky Way's eyelids flying,
Woi, Woi, let's also put on the sound of the path.

The path emerging from gingko trees is growing in gingko trees.
No end in sight.

Red Maple

Stubbornly, stubbornly,
the path goes roaming,
roaming, rubbing the sky's cheeks.

Stubbornly, stubbornly,
the path that has lost its way pounces,
the pathless path pounces

For You

I long to feed you
a bowl of rice warmed by my piping hot blood vessels.

An Anchor

A dark red anchor lay on the deck and said to me: Though
I floundered in the mud's embrace the sound of its heart was
    really beautiful

Vine Leaves

Two cicadas clasp the old tree's vine and cry

> One month, two months gathering blood, three months four
> months morning sickness

Brrrr Brrrr the sound of love trembling

Lighthouse Song

If your eyes can embrace a thousand *li*

If your eyes can embrace a thousand *li*
then sit around my rim

I will go,
will go a thousand *li* with you

In the Subway

Deep, deep down in the subway
young couples
secretly
attach and detach their lips
like lightning

So far

Hubba-hubba-hubba

A Wandering Star

> Bari is walking / Bari is walking / Spreading ocher skirts, a blue
> horizon / Past one corner between blue-green loaves / Past a
> second corner, between speckled red loaves / Bari is walking /
> Bari is walking

Eternity joyfully shook the night air. Everything in the house
shrank in surprise at the sound of eternity. Everything was connecting
up, to the dreams of sleep, the sleep of dreams, the table, the gas stove,
the clothes dryer, the computer, the separate garbage bins, the shelves,
the instant spicy seafood stew, even me.

> The face of night looked like a swollen loaf of bread. Soaps were
> joyfully connecting up, too. Borne on the back of a long, long
> shelf's back, packs of *ramyeon* were joyfully connecting up, too.
> Hugged by a drawer holding its breath waiting, coffee was joyfully
> connecting up, too.
> Bending its dried back, a shrimp was joyfully connecting up, too.

> Bari is walking / Bari is walking / Spreading ocher skirts, a blue
> horizon / Past one corner between blue-green loaves / Past a
> second corner, between speckled red loaves / Bari is walking /
> Bari is walking

Connecting is this star's virtue, or parting's virtue.

Having clung on to the end, a wandering star the color of hope, or a
repeat sign the color of hope

Song of Three Sisters

—For J.J.

> Unjo is walking / Unjo is walking / Spreading ocher skirts, a blue
> horizon / Past one corner carrying one song / past a second corner,
> carying a second song / past a third corner, into a third song / Unjo is
> walking. / Heart trembling, Unjo is walking.

You said you had walked with no end.
Looking at the water flowing along the banks
you must have been looking at the petals
appearing and disappearing in the water,
at the capillaries of their beautiful petals

Oh, God, Song, Send us the most familiar melodies.
We walked and walked last night and last day
so make the sorrows of all the windows leave us.

Make oblivion ripe within us.
Make shoes exchange good-bye kisses.
On these fields where heartrending prayers are wandering a
sound of fruits of recollection ripening,
a sound of gardens with a thousand paths picking up one leaf as they
      wander,
We all lying face down like affectionateslopes walking into mountain ranges,
lying there, endlessly spreading wings of song

Make the lamps wear wedding rings of eternity and sympathy on every
      stairway.
Winds arrive, arrive with no end,
Small birds sitting on violet-colored railings in gardens
stay awake through one night then one more night,
and as they wake they mature the wind's liquor.

You said you had walked with no end Looking
at the water flowing along the banks you must
have been looking at the petals appearing and

disappearing in the water,
at the capillaries of their beautiful petals

> Unjo is walking / Unjo is walking / Spreading ocher skirts,
> a blue horizon / Past one corner carrying one song / past a
> second corner, carying a second song / past a third corner,
> into a third song / Unjo is walking. / Heart trembling, Unjo
> is walking.

The Sound of Footsteps

> Unjo is walking / Unjo is walking / Spreading ocher skirts,
> a blue horizon / Past one corner between silver pans / past
> a second corner, between silver ladles / Unjo is walking. /
> Heart trembling, Unjo is walking.

Now it's time for him to come,
time for him to come dragging his travel bag full of sorrows
like the sound of each lonely footstep
in very narrow alleys
like the wrinkles in the sound of feet
now it's time for him to come,
a very deep underground cell beneath an ancient ceiling
beneath shaking windowsills

You are memories.
Your skin is the touch of loss.
Do not forget
how, when the stars came, the lanky window bars used to open
    their shoulders.

> Unjo is walking / Unjo is walking / Spreading ocher skirts,
> a blue horizon / Past one corner between silver pans / past
> a second corner, between silver ladles / Unjo is walking. /
> Heart trembling, Unjo is walking.

Pigweed jumped into boiling water even with such dissuasion
After warming up a little there
it will be lightly boiled.

Now it's time for him to come,
time for him to come dragging his travel bag full of sorrows.
An underground cell deep in dust like an afternoon's slumber,
    when he comes.

> Unjo is walking / Unjo is walking / Spreading ocher skirts,
> a blue horizon / past one corner, past two corners, Heart
> trembling, trembling.

The Floor's Song

Wiping the floor of my room, I mumble, Floor, I love you so much.

Make the road and go, make the road and go.

You are a flower You
are the void You are
the universe You are
history

Wiping the void, I mumble, Void, I love you so much.

Walk along the full void, walk along the full void.

An Empty Jar

Blue moonlight sinks down dizzy in the yard, in the corner of a sandy yard thorny plants painfully push their breasts forward, I stand embracing an empty jar to my chest.

Like a wrecked ship where wandering stars pause on their way, an exhausted body trapped in the sand up to the waist, a road fluttering

How can you leave, how can you leave?

For a Dance

That sky will never be able to put down a star.*
That toe of a padded sock will never be able to let go of a star.

> *Deongdeokkung Deongdeokkung Deongdeokkung To*
> *the beat of a ritual song, Deongdeokkung*

Tonight when all the thighs of freedom
will open without end,
hang a lamp at the tip of the eaves of ideals.

> *Dump it, dumper.*
> *Throw it, thrower.*
> *Dead or alive, You are gone for ever*

That sleep can never let go of dreams.
That roof rising roundly can never part from the wind

> *Deongdeokkung Deongdeokkung Deongdeokkung To the beat of*
> *a ritual song, Deongdeokkung*

*in memory of Choi Seunghee, a dancer in the Joseon Dynasty

Now Hold Out Your Hands

Now hold out your hand
You are your wrinkled hat
You are your loosened blood vessel
You are your amber-hued button
You are your golden liver ribs, uh-huh, uh-huh.

You are your hopeful azure athlete's foot
You are your trembling wound
You are your throat's truncated shadow
You are your cholesterol, uh-huh, uh-huh.

Now hold out your hand
You are your golden jacket
You are your unfocussed pupil You
are your gold-rimmed glasses
You are your fluttering hamburger, uh-huh, uh-huh.

You are your dreaming virus
You are a heart hibernating dangling from an electric pylon, dreaming of
    your most delicious blood,

Now hold out your hand, your sleep, your rotation, uh-huh, uh-huh, ah,
I will wait for the zodiac you hold out

A Stamen

What shall I do with those lights?
Those lights licking light, their bodies turned into eyes.

Eager to see, eager to see,

eager to see a stamen jumping down

Future

The island reflects politely.
Reflects politely hugging royal azaleas to a cliff breast.
Reflects politely with its feet immersed in cold water.

You, Future that was once mine

A Harbor

It is sleeting in the harbor.
A sound of footsteps passing the low chink in the door, a sound of crying
    in distant islands, a
sound of bubbles carrying whimpering waves on their backs.

It is sleeting.
Howl, shameful crabs, seaweed, baby octopus from the Cape of Hope,
    naked here all lie flat.
Climb up climb up
Howling, climb up

All dreams with their heads on a pillow turned toward islands,
All islands, turning their footsteps toward dreams.

You are the spine of dreams
You are the variability of dreams
You are the speeding of dreams.
Climb up, climb up
Even the soul, climb up, even the spirit, climb up

At Each Valley

Thrice three years
meeting one man in every single valley.
Thrice three years
meeting rapture in every second valley

An uphill path standing barefoot
The girl glimmering

    Eeru It's fate/yo-ho it's fate /yo-ho it's fate

Once a section of heart has opened like that,
a section of heart open on an icy pond like that

Soil

Tears giving birth to a child of tears
flapping flapping, giving birth to a child of tears

Like gravel holding flowing water tight,
like geese anxious to go flying off,
like thunderbolts stealthily kindling in folds of soil.

Soil, extinctions borne on the back of soil!
Sobbing sobbing births, speed of resurrection,

Tears, tears giving birth to a child,
flapping flapping, giving birth to a child of tears

A Slope

A slope sloping downward, flapping flapping a sound of gravel,
dizzy on a white wall, the dark shadow of a body with a sound of
    gravel borne on its back .
First it grows dark, going ahead, going ahead along a winding path, .
I follow along behind your shadow dancing,

A Couple's Laundry

The steaming iron is sliding hot and long over the stained window.
A page crumpled in the tears of the Apostles' Creed, Sunday flying
  between fleecy clouds,

Smartphone

There, so many foreheads were bowing in worship before salvation . . .

A Self-Service Gas Station

On the way to the Mandeok Tunnel, there is a gas station sitting like an old low wooden bench. The so-called Green gas station, some time after passing it, I see it has changed into a self-service gas station and is waving its hands. With a placard "fill up with happiness!" flying deep in the sky.

I too then took a self-placard from my bosom and set it flying. In the deep sky gracefully spreading the lyric's "shawl" over my shoulders

The lyric's,
"shawl" believing it to be the happiness of art.
The lyric's,
"shawl" believing it to be the happiness of beauty.
The lyric's,
"shawl" believing it to be the happiness of goodness.
The lyric's,
"shawl" believing it to be the happiness of the truth,

Etc, etc

Into the deep sky where black gasoline is happy too, painting its happy
    mouth dark
Flying many placards like funeral flags

A Vampire Building

I developed astigmatism. My eyes had astigmatism so my mind, too, had astigmatism. I misread 'maejang', the dazzling store in the mart, as 'maejang', the burial of a corpse, and misread the sign at one restaurant, 'twaeji-gogi-mu-jjigae' (Pork-daikon-stew) as 'twaeji mu-jjigae' (pig rainbow) (imagining a pig as a rainbow! such an original idea!) and I mistook the 'annae' (information) desk in the sparkling department store for the desk 'nae anui' (inside me) and was duly startled. I misread the poster caption 'World *Sagyeok* (Shooting) Tournament' as 'World *Sajeok* (History) Tournament' (Who is coming? Žižek? Baudrillard or Baudelaire? Benjamin or Jakobson? My heart was overflowing!) I misread 'Empire' building as 'Vampire' building (even wondering what 'Vampire' meant), I misread *silpae* (a reel of thread) as *silpae* meaning 'failure' (I even wrote it down in a poem!) and a remote *i seom* (island) as remote *iseong* (reason), *byul* (star) as *beol* (bee), *saram* (human) as *sarang* (love), no, vice versa·····

49

The Golden-Haired Tiger of 'Hotel Peninsula'

The Golden-Haired Tiger of 'Hotel Peninsula.' That was my name. At first, when I was kicked out of the circus, I danced in the hotel lobby. Then, having become the Golden-Haired Tiger of 'Hotel Peninsula,' I grew old surrounded by people as I chewed up the lumps of raw red meat someone threw at me. I, who once used to run riding the wind, like a bee changing its mind for a pine forest, changing its mind for a celandine, changing its mind for a grosbeak, escaping down distant dream roads.

> Floundering floundering
> floundering floundering

Then one spring day, a spring day tired of dancing, I was sent to a little garden in the Peninsula Coffee Shop, packing my flabby belly and lusterless golden hair away with my dreams. I, who once used to run riding the wind. I, who was once the last guardian spirit of the grasslands of Taeung Mountain.

> Floundering floundering
> floundering floundering

Now, people outside the plate glass window watch me prowling under dried maple branches soaking my golden hair in the artificial waterfall. A young keeper throws lumps of raw read meat at me and starts to sing: "The golden-haired tiger is gone, is gone. The golden-haired tiger of of Taeung Mountain that once used to run riding the wind is gone."

> Dappled dappled floundering floundering
> Dappled dappled floundering floundering

Redevelopment Loneliness

I walk along the redevelopment lane where a few streetlights are opening
  their eyes obliquely.
Sealed letters, not yet read, are sticking their heads out of mailboxes
while grimy flags, not yet lowered, are holding out flapping hands to the
  twlight sky.
Couches, their chests draped with black cotton stuffing like medals, like
  confessions, cups half-buried in sand, upside-down kettles, raucous
  weeds, bones of mirrors glistening like necklaces.
In the lamplight casting a circle of light only there a woman sitting at a
  sewing machine with orange plastic fluttering is pushing a black collar
  toward the needle.
An orange scarf on the back of her neck spread wide like a royal palace,
  where did I see her? She looks like the Virgin Mary.
Ruins sneaking along,
immortality nowhere,
everywhere hope overflowing, overflowing,
redevelopment loneliness growing silently.

I walk along the redevelopment lane where a few streetlights are coming
  on like resurrection.
I walk amidst the loneliness warm with streetlights, where the backs of
  vanishing things stretch long.
Immortality nowhere.
Everywhere hope overflowing, overflowing

Closer, yet Closer

I am socially disadvantaged.
You petals suspending shadows, closer, yet closer

I am a minority.
You lamps holding dawn in your mouths, closer, yet closer

You peaces, hopes that grow soft once here,
closer, yet closer

Older Sister Yeong-Ju

We called that woman Older Sister Yeong-Ju. Wearing a white poplin apron (with the sleeves of her newlywed bride's yellow *jeogori* firmly rolled up), now in her seventies, Older Sister Yeong-Ju used to be standing all alone at the kitchen door holding a pink flower-patterned plate of pale green pumpkin pancakes when we came home from school, that woman looking like a silhouette, Older Sister Yeong-Ju.

Today, holding an old-fashioned purse, turned into a round brick on the corner of a row-house's red wall, pitifully engraved as if a dream or reality, she might be stroking her once-kind life, or recalling her unfaithful husband. Taking care of her handsome husband, the woman so good with her needle that she was the talk of the town, Older Sister Yeong-Ju, her prominent lips have been worn down by time until they fit her face very prettily.

Still my little older sister, even in her seventies, how softly she fried her pale green pumpkin pancakes, it took her only a night to sew a jeogori, still following me and wrapping my hands in her pink mittens in winter, my sister, my sister, my lamplike sister, a woman pure as the white snow meantioned in Baek Seok's poems.

The snow-white backs of sister's hands where blue tendons flow like rivers, whisper, "Sister was a seamstress once. Whenever her needle pierced through, buttonholes suddenly grew fat and seams grew strong."

Suddenly raising her head,
On the red wall of row house, those speeding colored threads, silver needles tugging at variegated threads

We called that woman Older Sister Yeong-Ju. Wearing a white poplin apron (with the sleeves of her newlywed bride's yellow jeogori firmly rolled up), her silhouette rainbow-hued like dazzliing silk threads, that woman, Older Sister Yeong-Ju.

Jajangmyeon

The awkward posture of a man, kneeling upright on a cement floor, putting lolling jajangmyeon bowls in a steel container, edges colored blood-red, bowls (crimson noodles are still left in some or what look like half-eaten noodles stirred and swollen). He is clearly a saint of our times, kneeling more sincerely than any monk. Moreover, he bows his navy jacket like a monk's habit, while drop by drop raindrops are rolling down like monastic tears. He is praying.

Here is a cement sanctuary where the sounds of prayer resonate. Now the man will head for Golgotha, his arms spread wide like Jesus Christ, bearing a silvery steel container on his back. Riding a motorcycle, his golden hair fluttering behind his back, he will always only show his back. He will feed this age that noisily clamors hooting like thunder rolling near rainy lake Galilee. Ah, a bowl of jajangmyeon flying through the sky. It will rise again. It will rise again. A bowl of jajangmyeon.

Ah, The Things That Make Me
Write Poems Again Today

My fingers, too dull to type a capital T.
My convulsions, their why and when as yet unknown.
My lifelong lovers, lulling my convulsions to sleep – Dilantin and
    Valium, Tegretol, Lamictal, those round, white skins.
An ivory-colored fountain pen that a sick poet gave me, my
notebooks, diaries, books abandoned countless times,
a post-office counter visited at 4:30 pm, unposted green postcards, in
    the parcels section a brawny young man who looks like Reagan,
    demanding a signature,
corners safely passed one day, crosswalks without signal lights,
the arrows with projecting lips that I have met on streets here and there,
my smartphone note pad biting the remaining two years' installment as if
    biting the sorrow of surviving,
virgin-like, sad music,
the closed circuit of a silver picture-frame,
a subway heading for a secret sanctum, a school.

Automatic doors opening for anyone,
a gorgeous whore, freedom, democracy,
the future lying on its back whimpering,
latent flu,
the gleaming hats you wore, or the halo, or its abstract deferral,
the sincerity of melodramas, the eternity of brooches,
my recollections and hopes with their thick eye shadow.

And, and

Ah, met in this world, that

Dedicating to Myself

Now let's take them out.
From the dusty shelves of creased bosom
let's take out the wings
dressed in underwear of layers of ruins like fallen leaves

Meanwhile, I have too often critiqued criticism.
Meanwhile, I have too often absented the present.
Meanwhile, I have too often died death.
Meanwhile, I have too often talked about satellites.
Meanwhile, I have too often recollected recollections.
Meanwhile, I have heard too often the May songs of one with no May,

Meanwhile, I have only raged about thoroughfares. I have never raged
    about the yellow cat fur scattered like petals on thoroughfares.
I did not so much as glance at corners laying their hands on
    their bosoms.
I have purchased far too many postcards with nothing written on them.
    Without going to the post office, or without trying to find out how
    many addresses are looking for homes.

I never become a peach blossom near peach blossoms. I
took no care of noon's timeless shadow.
I took no care of footpaths winding holding their breath.
I only talked about a shining marble floor. I never talked about walls
    always leaking a little blood or about chairs' blood vessels.
I used to omit
postal numbers such as '278-1' attached to the steep hill of 'Jangmi-gil
    number 25.'
I never gave a glance at the bare light bulb one corner of a slanting
    ceiling was always waiting for.

The world is a fragment of a path.

On the slopes remaining yearned-for songs are wandering.
On the slopes too many shadows are eagerly waiting for summer
    afternoons.
On the slopes moonlit nights are clutching the steps.

Let's become peach blossom near peach blossoms.
Let's talk about the sweat-sodden back and damp weight of labor.

Ah, now let's talk
about the bare light bulb waiting for you in a corner far into the night.
Let's shut the drawer and wind white bandages round the body of agony.
Let's talk about roofs crouching low sheltering from the rain.

About trivial things.
About forgotten things.
About barely breathing things.

About viburnum,
About yellow-billed grosbeaks and buttercups.
So let the windows of the sanctuary open in the morning
and in the evening let kindly birds hang their wings on violet clouds and
    ardently wave their legs

Then, and then, and then.

I am a duck crying somewhere.
Crab apples, harmonizing their breathing, celebrate my wings, celebrate
    my ₩30,000 poem.

Seomyun

> Bari is walking / Bari is walking / Spreading ocher skirts, a
> blue horizon / Past one corner between arrows / Past a second
> corner, between arrows / Bari is walking / Heart trembling,
> Bari is walking

That lamp inside the fluttering dusk,
those tears not wiped from between torn pages,
traces of tears are deep, those golden coat-strings.

Between, between fluttering, fluttering wisteria tunnels,
between, between bending roads,
between, between that death hesitating at the sound of life's alarm,
gazing around and around.

Passing wooden walls with eyes barely open.

As if seeing, not seeing, not seeing

Passing the too vast heavenly realm,
distant things seem close,
close things are far far away.

Walking walking through writhing hope,
Walking walking through salvation, those distant lips

> Bari is walking / Bari is walking / Spreading ocher skirts, a
> blue horizon / Past one corner between arrows / Past a second
> corner, between arrows / Bari is walking / Heart trembling,
> Bari is walking

The Woman in Tula

That woman in Tula who used to blush,
that woman in Tula who used to ask the menu carefully, that
woman who used to put on a red-apple-patterned apron
and make red salad,
the sunset which used to come running, when she smiled carefully,
the woman in Tula who used to turn over and wipe the reddened tables,
that woman of red glasses, red curtains, red calculator

When she pushes open the thick glass door
shyness comes bubbling up the spiral stairs.

The Family Photo of Mr. Taejoon Lee 1

The novelist Mr. Taejoon Lee stands in the middle, holding a child with
     lowered head,
a boy with a crewcut is frowning, his hands behind his back,
a long-faced woman in white jacket and black skirt,
and next to her a girl next to her a girl and the old stairs of the storage
     terrace a maple tree an open window and an aster

Might he come now, into the crooked maple tree in front of the storage
     terrace,
into the crooked asters in front of the storage terrace?

Free Verse Editions

Edited by Jon Thompson

13 ways of happily by Emily Carr
& in Open, Marvel by Felicia Zamora
At Your Feet (A Teus Pés) by Ana Cristina César, edited by Katrina
    Dodson, translated by Brenda Hillman and Helen Hillman
Bari's Love Song by Kang Eun-Gyo, translated by Chung Eun-Gwi
Between the Twilight and the Sky by Jennie Neighbors
Blood Orbits by Ger Killeen
The Bodies by Christopher Sindt
The Book of Isaac by Aidan Semmens
Canticle of the Night Path by Jennifer Atkinson
Child in the Road by Cindy Savett
Condominium of the Flesh by Valerio Magrelli, translated by
    Clarissa Botsford
Contrapuntal by Christopher Kondrich
Country Album by James Capozzi
The Curiosities by Brittany Perham
Current by Lisa Fishman
Day In, Day Out by Simon Smith
Dear Reader by Bruce Bond
Dismantling the Angel by Eric Pankey
Divination Machine by F. Daniel Rzicznek
Erros by Morgan Lucas Schuldt
Fifteen Seconds without Sorrow by Shim Bo-Seon, translated by Chung
    Eun-Gwi and Brother Anthony of Taizé
The Forever Notes by Ethel Rackin
The Flying House by Dawn-Michelle Baude
Go On by Ethel Rackin
Instances: Selected Poems by Jeongrye Choi, translated by Brenda
    Hillman, Wayne de Fremery, & Jeongrye Choi
The Magnetic Brackets by Jesús Losada, translated by Michael Smith
    & Luis Ingelmo
Man Praying by Donald Platt
A Map of Faring by Peter Riley
The Miraculous Courageous by Josh Booton
No Shape Bends the River So Long by Monica Berlin & Beth Marzoni
Not into the Blossoms and Not into the Air by Elizabeth Jacobson
Overyellow, by Nicolas Pesquès, translated by Cole Swensen

Physis by Nicolas Pesquès, translated by Cole Swensen
Pilgrimage Suites by Derek Gromadzki
Pilgrimly by Siobhán Scarry
Poems from above the Hill & Selected Work by Ashur Etwebi, translated by Brenda Hillman & Diallah Haidar
The Prison Poems by Miguel Hernández, translated by Michael Smith
Puppet Wardrobe by Daniel Tiffany
Quarry by Carolyn Guinzio
remanence by Boyer Rickel
Rumor by Elizabeth Robinson
Settlers by F. Daniel Rzicznek
Signs Following by Ger Killeen
Small Sillion by Joshua McKinney
Split the Crow by Sarah Sousa
Spine by Carolyn Guinzio
Spool by Matthew Cooperman
Summoned by Guillevic, translated by Monique Chefdor & Stella Harvey
Sunshine Wound by L. S. Klatt
System and Population by Christopher Sindt
These Beautiful Limits by Thomas Lisk
They Who Saw the Deep by Geraldine Monk
The Thinking Eye by Jennifer Atkinson
This History That Just Happened by Hannah Craig
An Unchanging Blue: Selected Poems 1962–1975 by Rolf Dieter Brinkmann, translated by Mark Terrill
Under the Quick by Molly Bendall
Verge by Morgan Lucas Schuldt
The Wash by Adam Clay
We'll See by Georges Godeau, translated by Kathleen McGookey
What Stillness Illuminated by Yermiyahu Ahron Taub
Winter Journey [Viaggio d'inverno] by Attilio Bertolucci, translated by Nicholas Benson
Wonder Rooms by Allison Funk

About the Author

Kang Eun-Gyo was born in Hongwon, Hamgyeongnamdo in 1945 and raised in Seoul. She got her bachelor's degree in English Literature and PhD in Korean Literature from Yonsei University. She made her literary debut with the publication of "Night of the Pilgrims" which earned her the 1968 New Writer Prize by the journal *Sasanggye* (World of Thoughts). Her most significant poetry collections are *House of Nothingness, Diary of a Pauper, House of Noises, Red Rivers, Song of the Wind*, and *Letter in the Wall*. Kang was also the recipient of the Korean Writers Prize and the Contemporary Literature Award.

About the Translator

Chung Eun-Gwi is Professor in the Department of English Literature at Hankuk University of Foreign Studies, Seoul. She received her PhD in Poetics at SUNY Buffalo in 2005. Her publications include *Ah, Mouthless Things* (2017), *Fifteen Seconds without Sorrow* (2016), *The Colors of Dawn: Twentieth Century Korean Poetry* (2016), and *When the Wind Blows* (2019). She has also published many articles and translations in various journals including *In/Outside: English Studies in Korea, World Literature Today, Cordite*, and *Azalea: Journal of Korean Literature and Culture*.

www.ingramcontent.com/pod-product-compliance
Lightning Source LLC
Chambersburg PA
CBHW022040090426
42741CB00007B/1141